FOREVER A CATERPILLAR

The story of a *beautiful* child

Written By

Candi C. P. Perry

Photos by Candi C. P. Perry

ISBN 978-1-4583-7487-5

9 781458 374875

"If a man does not keep pace with his companions, perhaps it is because he hears a different drummer. Let him step to the music which he hears, however measured or far away."

Henry David Thoreau
1817-1862

When I first started writing this book I felt like I was going to be competing in a world that I was completely unfamiliar with. I felt completely unlike an author, or writer. I felt like someone whose book would be tossed in a pile with many other unknown authors. I felt like I didn't have what it takes to be a great writer or a writer who would be remembered for many years. Mentally I prepared myself for taking on the task of writing this book by convincing myself that I had to share my story with the world for the benefit of the hundreds of thousands of children who have been damaged by simple words that stayed in their minds and hearts as a child and enslaved them into what seemed a world of hopelessness.

Hopeful   Helpless

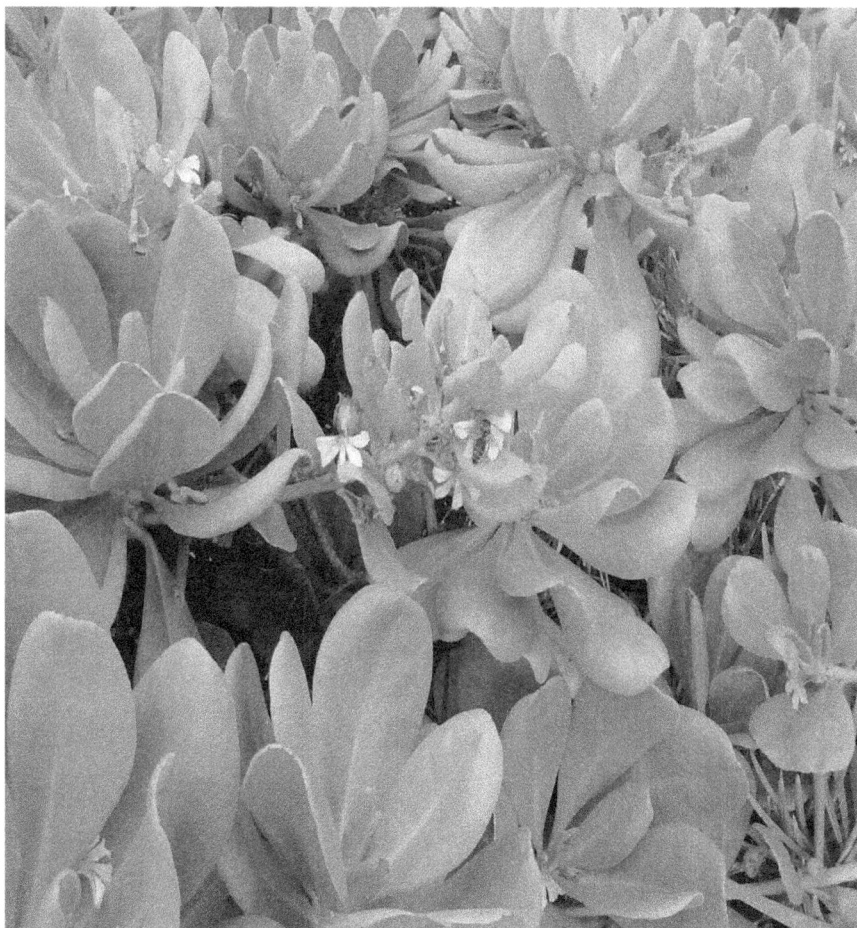

I was very nervous when I sat down for the first time to write this book. I realized that this book is actually a story reduced to ink on paper with pictures for others to see and learn from. I started feeling very much at ease and the thrill of telling my story began to arise. From that moment on the book began to come to life and I started my journey into the world of story-telling on paper.

Acknowledgements

I thank my lovely and wonderful Children, John-Payton, Keane, & Ariel Rowley for their joy, patience and understanding with all the many adventures I've taken them on and for being such a tremendous inspiration to my life. To the three of you, I thank you so much for being there for me through all of my pains and all of my joys. I thank my mother Viola for being one of the most beautiful butterflies among all the flowers of the world and for being a constant reminder that beauty is far more than outward appearance. I thank Vincent Burke a published author who himself has an amazing and inspiring story of a true experience of survival, and who through his own book writing and publishing has given me the inspiration and motivation for publishing this book. Vincent, thank you for not throwing the towel in on your profession when you didn't get the credit, awards, and honor that you were due so that you could be here for people like me. I thank LeEtta Davenport a woman who has dedicated her life to making a positive difference in the lives of young people, for reaching out to me and giving me an opportunity to share some of my many life stories with the youth of our Community. I am also giving a special thank you to Attorney Robert Turner who gave me the constant encouragement to keep my head up and to keep smiling when the world seemed dark and it seemed like there was no place else to go except back into the cocoon that had been locked away so many years ago. Thank you all for every wonderful part you have played in my life.

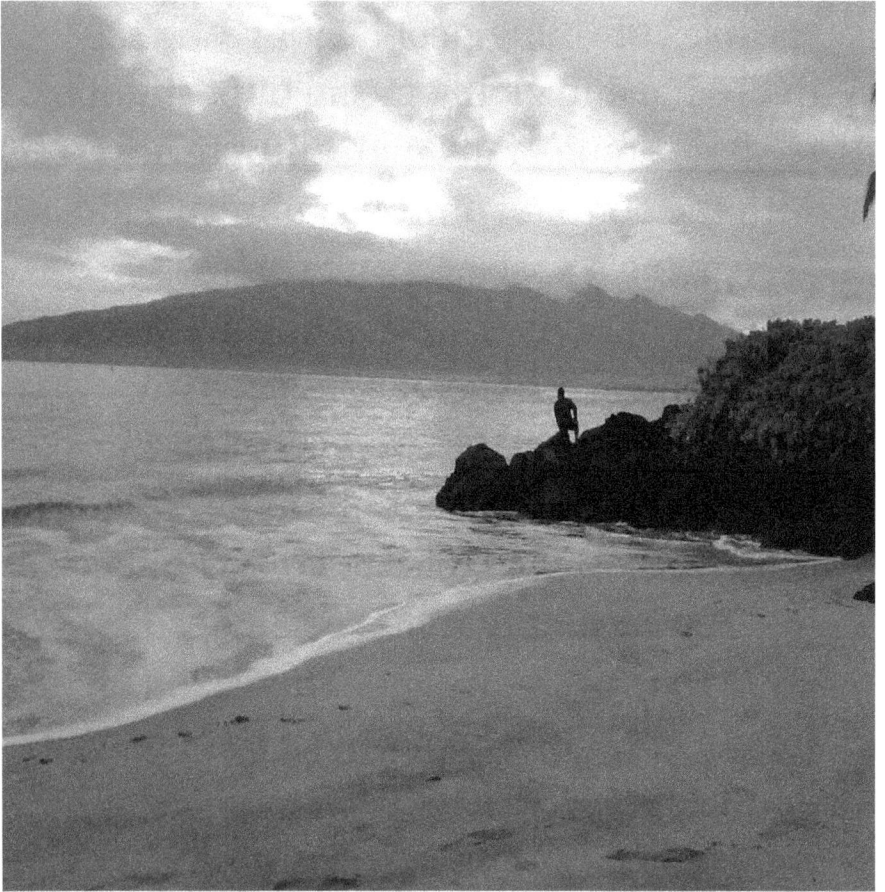

The focus of this book is to show how prejudice can affect the person to whom the prejudice is directed, and also the person who holds the prejudice. I hope that in showing this, the reader will become aware of the many aspects of a person's character and life that can be affected by prejudice. Most importantly, I hope that in reading this book the reader will be taken into the thoughts and emotions of the individuals who have been harmed by prejudice. By doing this, hopefully the reader will become more aware of the prejudices in his or her own life, and do whatever is necessary to rid themselves of them.

It all started at Grandview Elementary School, the place I looked forward to going everyday as a child. I had always enjoyed school and felt there was no place more comforting to be than in my classroom. A typical, beautiful and happy little girl growing up in a suburban neighborhood, I didn't want for anything. Subconsciously, I believed that I had the perfect life. The fantasy world I lived in kept me vibrant and always smiling. The world that every little girl in America dreams of having but only few actually live out was the life that I lived.Then there was Joey. Joey was one

of my classmates. He was very handsome and also an incredible athlete. He played football and was one of the fastest track and field runners. He had beautiful skin and a fantastic smile. His hair was just nappy enough for him to be considered a complete black boy, and just wavy enough to get the attention of all the girls in the classroom. Joey was also very smart. He made it known to everybody that he was going to play football in a professional team someday and that he was going to be a star quarter-back. I had the biggest crush on him. He was so friendly to everybody, one of the most talkative, nicest guys in the school. He

had a beautiful smile. Joey had the type of smile that made all the girls softly whisper to each other "ooooh, did you see him smile at me?" I had wished so many times that he would talk to me like he did the other girls and guys, or even look at me and smile, but he never did. Knowing that there was nothing wrong with me, I just figured that he didn't really notice me because I was so shy. Maybe he didn't want to bother me since I was always reading or concentrating on my class work. One day while we were at recess I told one of my classmates that I really liked Joey. She promised me that

she wouldn't tell anyone but she immediately ran across the grass and told some other classmates what I told her. I noticed them all snickering and laughing. They were putting their hands to their mouths like what she was telling them was the funniest thing they had ever heard. With my feelings hurt, I turned around, walked to the door, and sat down. My heart felt sad. I felt like I had done something terribly wrong by confiding in her. I don't know why I told her what I felt about Joey anyway. She wasn't a friend but I guess I felt like she was the closest one to it. She was the only girl who ever said "Hi" to me in class. I

didn't have any friends but I was such a happy little girl that it didn't matter if I had friends or not. Later that day in gym class I noticed everyone was in a group, except for me. Suddenly the whole class started to walk in my direction. I got excited thinking that they were going to present me with some sort of award, or sing a song to me, or maybe something even more exciting. My heart started to flutter and I burst out with the biggest smile a person could ever see. One of the girls ran up to me out of the group and reminded me of what I had said to my classmate earlier in the day at recess. The whole class then gathered around me and someone proclaimed, "Well, Joey has something he wants to tell you and he wants everyone to hear it". Then someone yelled out "Ok Joey, come tell her!" My heart raced faster. Finally, he was going to talk to me. My patience had paid off. He wanted me to be his friend. Every little girl's dream was to be friends with the stud of the classroom. I felt like I was in the midst of being presented with the crown for the Miss America Pageant.

As he walked toward me, he smiled at me from ear to ear. He looked at everyone else, and then at me again. He walked up really close to me and I said "Hi Joey", as I giggled and blushed, like most girls do when they don't know what else to do. Then the moment came. Everyone stood silent, motionless, and breathless. He spoke. My heart almost melted. I froze solid. I couldn't breathe. I just stared into his beautiful brown eyes.

"You are so stupid and ugly! Four-eyes, I would never like you. You're too fat and ugly, and you can't even climb a gym rope because you're so fat and ugly! You make me sick! Uuuggghhh!!" He then spit on the floor next to my feet, almost hitting my shoes with it. I stood motionless. I couldn't believe what had just happened. The inside of my throat felt like it was swelling to the point I was struggling to maintain consciousness. My heart was non-existent. I just stared into his eyes, as he stared into mine. I tried desperately to hold back the tears that were pushing against the back of my eyelids like a raging flood of blood. All my insides felt as though they were trying to make their way up through my throat that still seemed to be swelling. After a few minutes of glaring at me, he turned and walked away.

Everyone burst out in laughter as they pointed at me and walked away with him. A few voices rang above the rest as they conversed among themselves walking to the other side of the gymnasium "She is fat and ugly". I went and sat down on the bleachers. I was alone. There were many times when I had been by myself, but never felt alone. My life was forever changed. I was embarrassed and ashamed. I was fat. I wasn't attractive at all. I was extremely shy, a true fifth grade introvert. I wore glasses. These things had never raised a thought in my head before now. The rest of the day I was a walking corpse. When I arrived home at the end of the day, I went to the side of the house where no one could see me. While leaning on the side of the house, I cried like I had never before cried in my whole young life. I didn't know a person could cry so much. I didn't know a person could feel so much pain. The desire to no longer want

to be in existence was ripping at my soul.
From that day forth I kept my feelings
about what had happened, a secret. I
became very insecure about my looks
and who I was as a person. As time went
by I tried to make sense out of it, and I
concluded that he treated me like that
not only because I was fat, ugly, four-
eyed, and stupid, but also because of the
fact that I revealed that I liked him was
poison to his image. I never expected him
to be so mean, so cruel. His words rang
out in my mind and heart for what
seemed like hundreds of years.
During the years that followed I

rarely would let a male know how I felt deep inside for fear of rejection. I had never thought about my looks and how people perceived me until this point.

I was destined, to live a life in complete isolation and fear.

Twenty years later, as I was grocery shopping at a local grocery store, I noticed a man trying to get my attention. I ignored him, because I was in a rush to get home to feed my children. The man tried several times to talk to me, and to get my phone number. The man stated that he would like to take me out to lunch, or dinner sometime. I started smiling because he was so insistent and continued to tell me how gorgeous I was and how he felt I had a "bomb" body. For some reason, this particular day I was dressed extremely well for grocery shopping. He was a fat man, and not very handsome. He looked like a good bath, weight loss program, and shave would do a lot to help his physical appearance. He seemed run down, like maybe he had led a hard life. As I looked at him, he had a very familiar appearance that I could not seem to place.

 After several attempts with no success in getting me to participate in a conversation with him, I said "Thank you for the compliments and offers, but no thank you", and proceeded to walk away. Finally, he blurted out "Hey, aren't you Candi? Don't you remember me?" I said "No". He then told me who he was and he was excited about reminding me that we had gone to grade school together. My disposition completely changed.

It was Joey. He continued to tell me how beautiful I had become and asked me again if I would give him my number and let him take me out sometime. I couldn't believe what I was hearing. I felt the pain from 20 years ago come back all over again. As I looked at him I could hear the cold, cruel words he spoke to me as a child coming out of his mouth all over again, and again, as though he were speaking them at that very moment. I could see and hear the heartless laughter of my fifth grade classmates. It seemed like a lifetime was passing. The grocery store in which we stood took on the form and scenery of my elementary school playground, and gymnasium. Mentally, I was thrown back in time. I started thinking about the twenty years of damage this person, who had now become a man, had caused to my life.

My thoughts were interrupted by, "Excuse me. Did I say something wrong?" I shook my head, half-heartedly, smiled, and walked away. He called after me and I continued to walk away as though slowly waking from a dream.

After I left the grocery store I felt a sense of relief. I felt like a small piece of justice had been served. The tables had turned on Joey. I don't think he remembered even a small portion of what he had said and done to me twenty years before, but it really didn't matter. The damage had been done. Now, the one time superstar is physically unattractive, very lonely, and desperately wanting a lady like me to be his friend.

Joey's prejudice toward and against me had a lifelong effect on me. It changed the way I viewed men, thoughts, and emotions. It changed how I accepted compliments and gifts. It changed my desires, hopes and dreams. Most importantly it affected how I viewed and still view myself. To this day I many times doubt my attractiveness, intelligence, and the beauty of my body. Even though the table's had turned after twenty years, and Joey was now the one rejected, isolated, and unattractive, the pain he caused me remains. Although I know that inwardly I am a beautiful and very intelligent woman, I hope to someday be a butterfly and let my beauty fly free.

For now, I fear I will remain forever a caterpillar.

www.ingramcontent.com/pod-product-compliance
Lightning Source LLC
Chambersburg PA
CBHW021922040426
42448CB00007B/868